Learn
How to Draw
Activities for Kids Activity Book

Creative PlayBooks

This is your practice drawing space. Draw the images from the previous page here!
Find Other Great Titles By searching for <u>Creative Playbooks</u> on Your Favorite Book Retailer
Amazon.Com | Barnes & Noble (BN.Com) | Books A Million (BAM.Com)

This is your practice drawing space. Draw the images from the previous page here!
Find Other Great Titles By searching for <u>Creative Playbooks</u> on Your Favorite Book Retailer
Amazon.Com | Barnes & Noble (BN.Com) | Books A Million (BAM.Com)

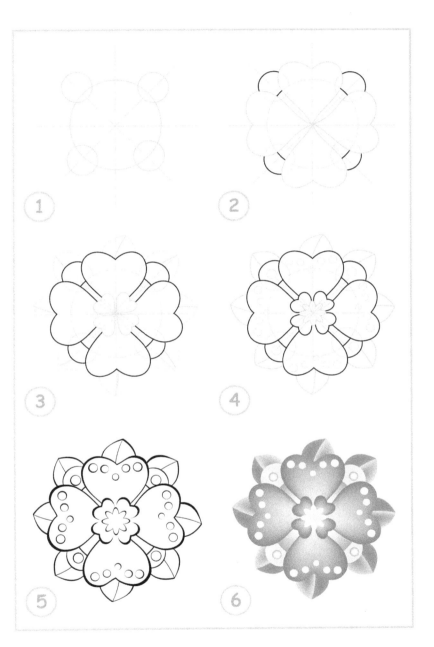

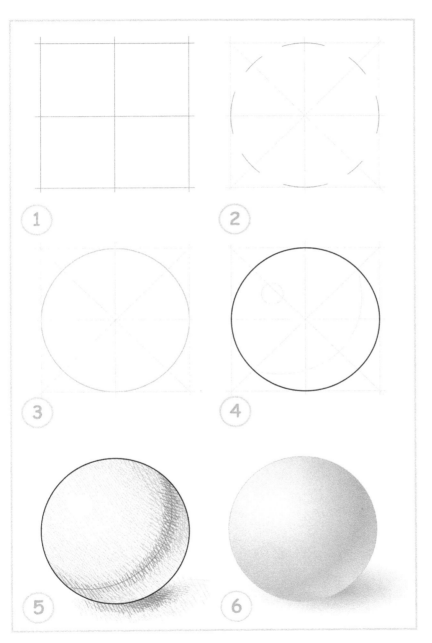

1

2

3

4

5

6

This is your practice drawing space. Draw the images from the previous page here!
Find Other Great Titles By searching for _Creative Playbooks_ on Your Favorite Book Retailer
Amazon.Com | Barnes & Noble (BN.Com) | Books A Million (BAM.Com)

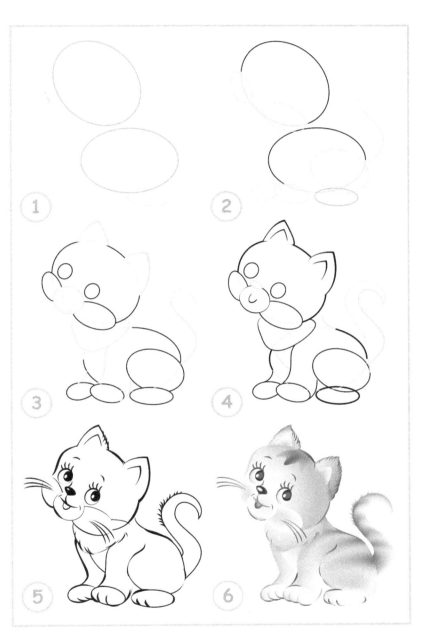

This is your practice drawing space. Draw the images from the previous page here!
Find Other Great Titles By searching for Creative Playbooks on Your Favorite Book Retailer
Amazon.Com | Barnes & Noble (BN.Com) | Books A Million (BAM.Com)

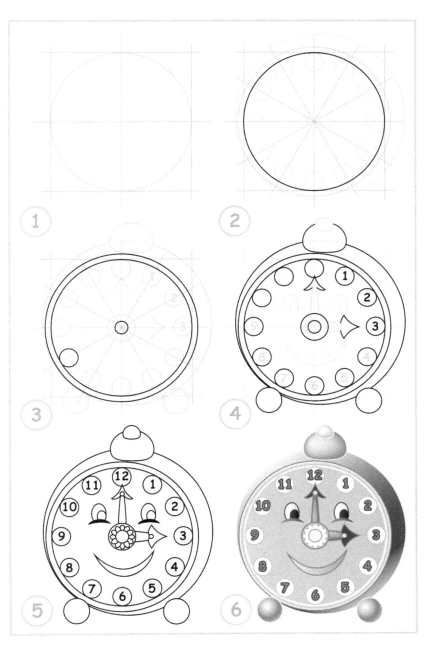

This is your practice drawing space. Draw the images from the previous page here!
Find Other Great Titles By searching for _Creative Playbooks_ on Your Favorite Book Retailer
Amazon.Com | Barnes & Noble (BN.Com) | Books A Million (BAM.Com)

INSTRUCTIONS FOR DRAWING:

THIS HOW-TO DRAWING BOOK CONSISTS OF IMAGES THAT ARE PLACED ON GRIDS. THERE IS AN EMPTY DRAWING BOX WITH GRIDS THAT WILL SERVE AS YOUR PRACTICE SPACE. TO COPY EACH IMAGE, DRAW PARTS OF THE IMAGE PER GRID AND PUT THEM ON THE BLANK GRIDS. SOUNDS DIFFICULT? NOT REALLY. TRY IT FIRST!

IT'S OKAY IF YOU DON'T COPY THE IMAGE PERFECTLY. AFTER ALL, DRAWING IS ABOUT THE EXPRESSION OF YOUR PERCEPTION AS WELL AS YOUR HAND STRENGTH AND CONTROL.

WHEN YOU'VE COPIED THE IMAGE, GO AHEAD AND COLOR IT NEXT! WE'RE EXCITED TO SEE WHAT YOU CAN DO!

DRAW THE IMAGE

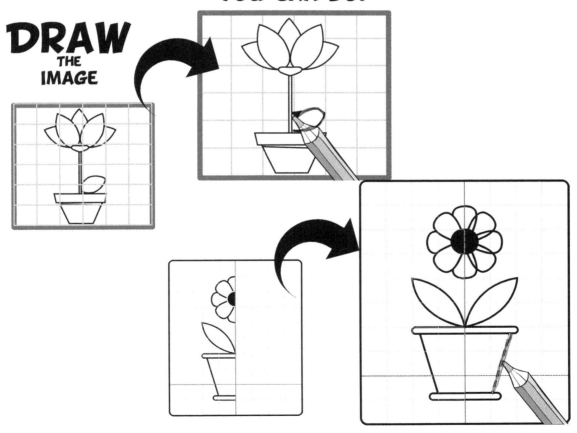

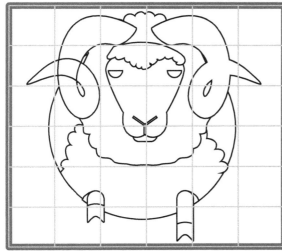

DRAW
THE
IMAGE

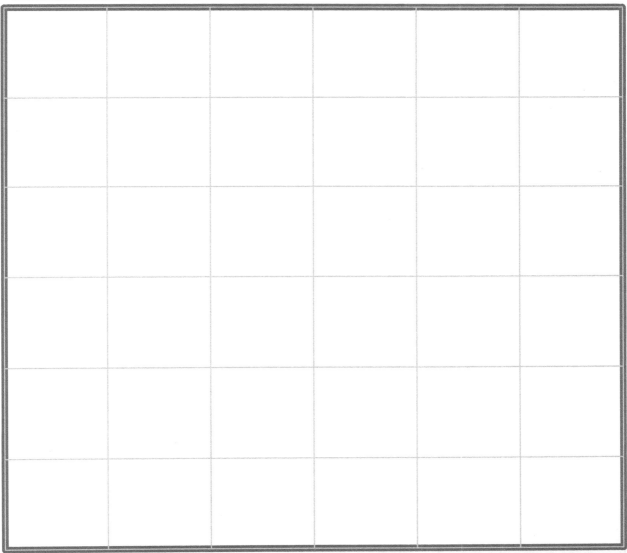

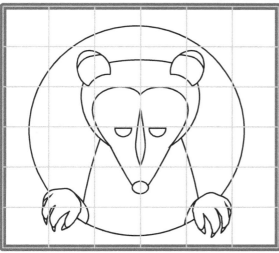

DRAW
THE
IMAGE

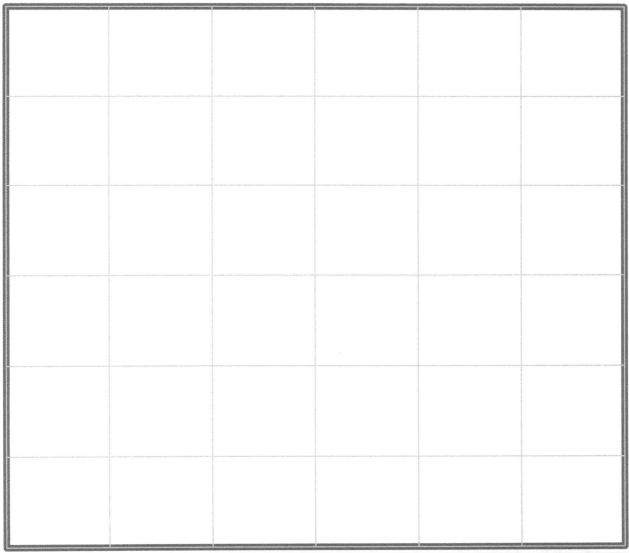

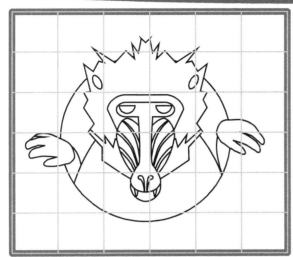

DRAW
THE
IMAGE

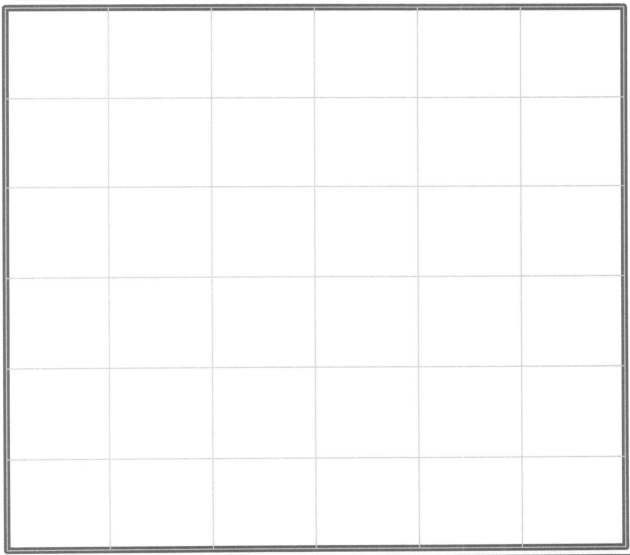

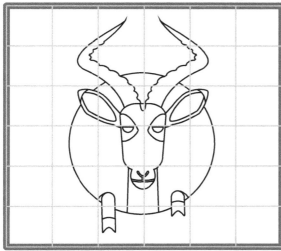

DRAW
THE
IMAGE

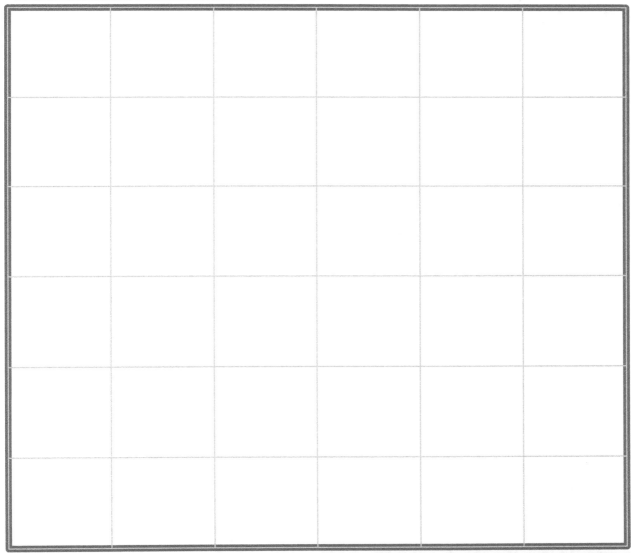

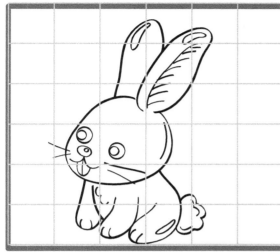

DRAW
THE
IMAGE

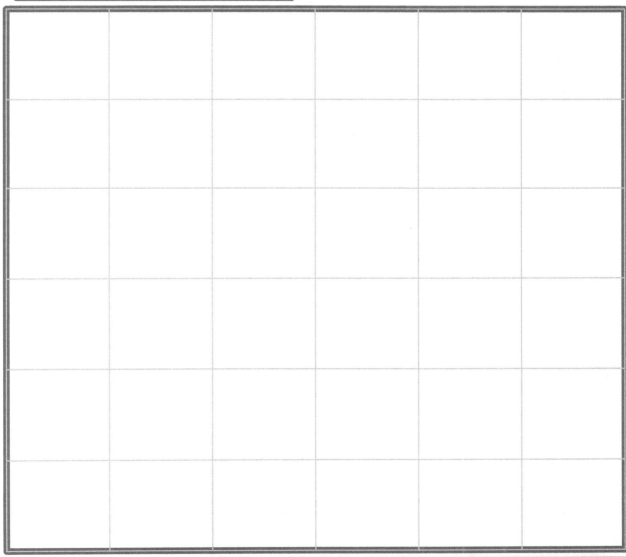

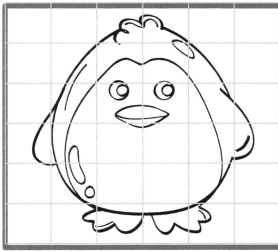

DRAW
THE
IMAGE

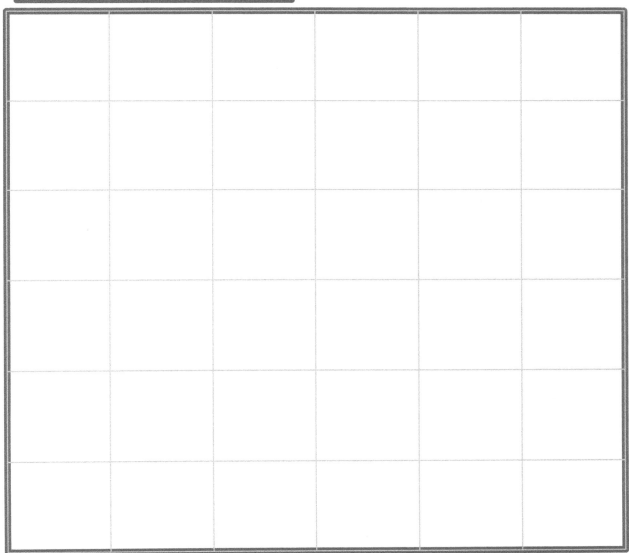

DRAW
THE
IMAGE

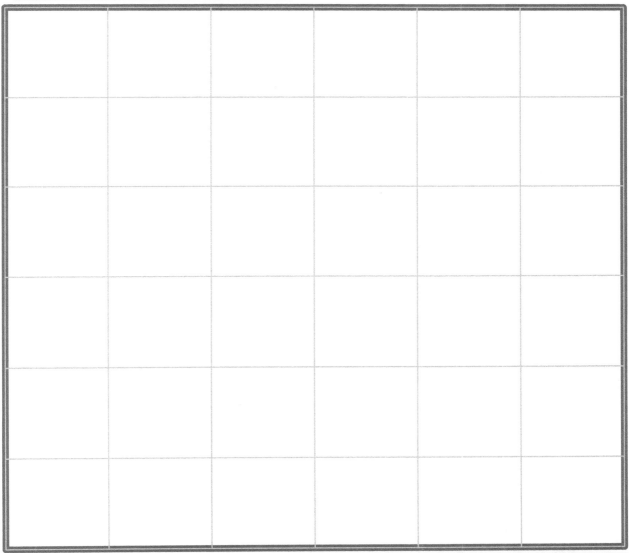

DRAW
THE
IMAGE

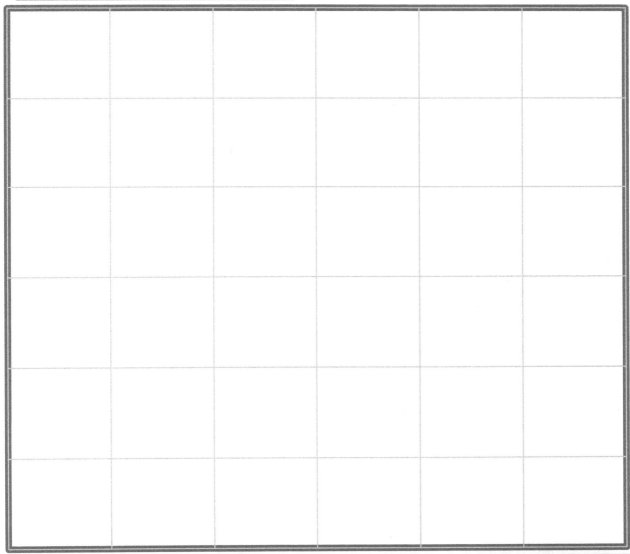

DRAW
THE
IMAGE

DRAW
THE
IMAGE

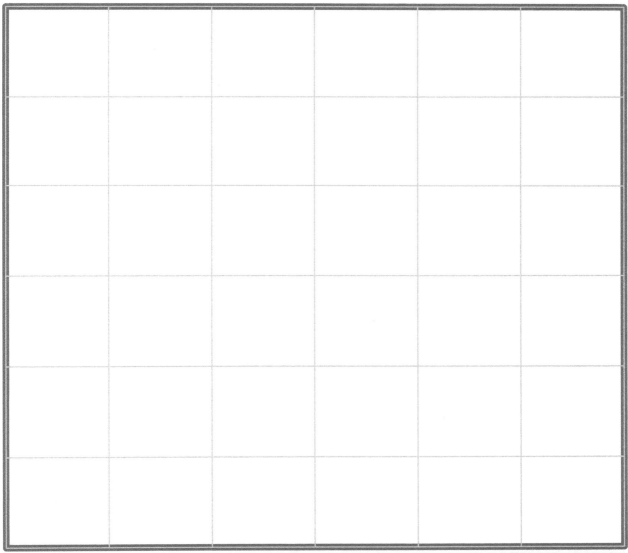

DRAW
THE
IMAGE

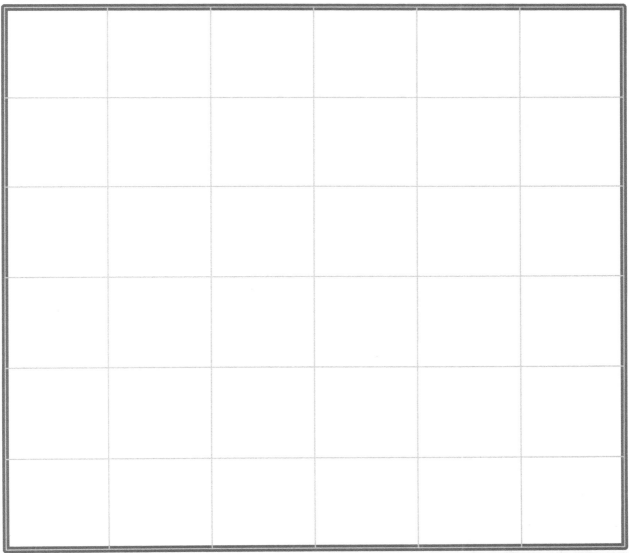

DRAW
THE
IMAGE

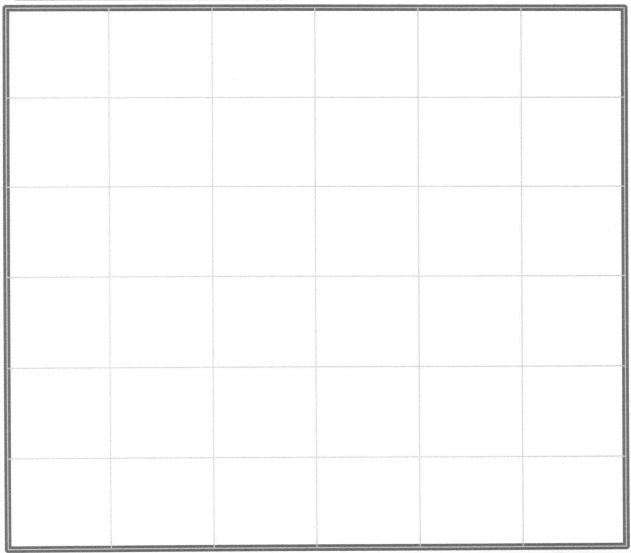

CPSIA information can be obtained
at www.ICGtesting.com
Printed in the USA
LVHW042014091118
596156LV00005B/157